5/04

EDGE BOOKS™

WAR MACHINES REMOTELY PILOTED AIRCRAFT

The Predators

By Michael and Gladys Green

Consultant:

Cyndi Wegerbauer
Public Relations Manager
General Atomics Aeronautical Systems Inc.
San Diego, California

Capstone press

Mankato, Minnesota

Edge Books are published by Capstone Press
151 Good Counsel Drive, P.O. Box 669, Mankato, Minnesota 56002
www.capstonepress.com

Library of Congress Cataloging-in-Publication Data
Green, Michael, 1952–
    Remotely piloted aircraft: the Predators / by Michael and Gladys Green.
    p. cm.—(Edge books. War machines)
    Summary: Describes the Predator, an unmanned aerial vehicle used by the United
States Air Force for surveillance and ground attacks, including its development,
equipment, weapons, and future military use.
    Includes bibliographical references and index.
    ISBN 0-7368-2417-0 (hardcover)
    1. Predator (Drone aircraft)—Juvenile literature. 2. Hellfire (Guided missile)—
Juvenile literature. [1. Predator (Drone aircraft) 2. Hellfire (Guided missile)
3. Reconnaissance aircraft. 4. Guided missiles. 5. Aerial reconnaissance.] I. Green,
Gladys, 1954– II. Title. III. Series.
UG1242.D7G74 2004
623.7'469—dc22   2003012560

Editorial Credits
Carrie Braulick, editor; Jason Knudson, designer; Jo Miller, photo researcher

Photo Credits
General Atomics Aeronautical Systems Inc., 5, 11, 12, 13, 16–17, 19, 22–23, 25
Getty Images Inc./AFP, cover; David McNew, 29; U.S. Air Force, 26
NASA Dryden Flight Research Center Photo Collection/GA-ASI/Alan Waide, 15
Photo by Ted Carlson/Fotodynamics, 21
U.S. Air Force photo by Tech. Sgt. Scott Reed, 9
U.S. Marine Corps photo by Chief Warrant Officer William D. Crow, 6

1 2 3 4 5 6 09 08 07 06 05 04

Table of Contents

CHAPTER 1

The Predator in Action

Late one summer night, enemy soldiers meet at a small fort in the mountains. They are planning to attack a nearby U.S. military base. They do not know that a U.S. Air Force MQ-1 Predator is quietly flying above them.

Hundreds of miles away, an Air Force crew operates the Predator from a control station on the ground. The crew watches the enemy soldiers on a screen.

After the meeting, the enemy commander drives away in the darkness. He plans to return to his secret command post. The Predator follows his car.

LEARN ABOUT:

The commander arrives at the command post. The Predator points a beam of light at the building. The post explodes in a huge fireball. The Predator flies back to its ground station.

Predators entered Air Force service in 1995.

Background

In the early 1990s, General Atomics Aeronautical Systems Inc. (GA-ASI) designed the RQ-1 Predator for the Air Force. With the unmanned aircraft, the Air Force could watch military action around the world. At the same time, they could keep aircraft crews a safe distance from the battlefield. A crew flies the Predator from the ground instead of from inside the aircraft.

In 1994, the Air Force received its first RQ-1 Predators. By 1995, the Predators were in service. The Air Force flew them on at least 600 missions that year.

In early 2001, GA-ASI put air-to-ground missiles on some Predators. These Predators are called MQ-1s. Later that year, the first Predator missiles were fired at targets in Afghanistan. In 2003, the Air Force flew MQ-1s to spy on the Iraqi military during Operation Iraqi Freedom.

CHAPTER 2

Inside the Predator

Today, the Air Force has about 90 Predators. Predators fly on missions throughout the world.

The Predator is smaller than most aircraft. It is about 27 feet (8.2 meters) long. It has a wingspan of 48.7 feet (14.8 meters).

A crew operates the Predator from a ground control station (GCS). The GCS is built into a large trailer.

Engine

A Rotax 914 gasoline engine powers the Predator. The engine gives the Predator a top speed of about 170 miles (274 kilometers) per hour.

The Predator can travel about 460 miles (740 kilometers) without refueling. It can stay in the air for 40 hours.

Crews test the Predator's parts before it flies on missions.

LEARN ABOUT:

Cameras

The Predator's equipment helps it spy on enemy forces. For these reconnaissance missions, the aircraft may carry equipment that weighs as much as 450 pounds (204 kilograms).

The flight crew in the GCS sees the views from the Predator's cameras. The GCS crew receives the images in less than a second. A color camera is in the Predator's nose. The view from this camera allows the pilot in the GCS to fly the aircraft.

Three cameras are in a compartment that hangs below the Predator's nose. Two video cameras produce clear images in daylight. The flight crew uses the forward-looking infrared (FLIR) camera to see the aircraft's surroundings at night. This camera senses temperature differences between objects. The objects appear on a screen in the GCS.

Other Equipment

The Predator can be equipped with a radar system. The flight crew uses the system when clouds, smoke, or haze blocks the vision of the cameras. It shows a black-and-white image in the GCS.

The MQ-1 Predator has a laser designator that helps missiles hit targets. The designator sends out laser light to a target. Missiles then follow the path of the laser light.

The MQ-1 also can launch smaller remotely piloted aircraft. These aircraft can sense harmful chemicals in the air.

Three cameras are located beneath the Predator's nose.

GCS Equipment

The GCS has two 20-inch (51-centimeter) color TV screens. The upper screen shows a map of the target area. The lower screen shows a view from the Predator's nose camera and flight instrument readings. Instrument readings show speed, altitude, fuel levels, and other information.

The GCS is inside a large trailer.

Screens in the GCS show images from the Predator's cameras.

The GCS includes a satellite system called the Trojan Spirit II. This system includes two satellite dishes mounted on the trailer. The Trojan Spirit II allows the crew to send the Predator's camera images anywhere in the world.

GCS Crew

The GCS usually has several crew members. A pilot uses a control stick and throttle to take off, land, and control the Predator in flight. The pilot sometimes allows an autopilot system to control the Predator. The autopilot system keeps the Predator flying on course at a certain altitude.

The flight crew also includes two or three sensor operators. The sensor operators control the video cameras, radar system, and weapons.

NASA's Altair

Remotely piloted aircraft have been an important part of the Air Force since the early 1990s. During this time, the National Aeronautics and Space Administration (NASA) also wanted to fly remotely piloted aircraft.

NASA formed the Environmental Research Aircraft and Sensor Technology (ERAST) program. Through ERAST, NASA develops remotely piloted aircraft for scientific studies.

One of ERAST's newest aircraft is the Altair. The Altair's design is based on the latest Predator model, the Predator B. But the two aircraft have some differences. The Altair has a larger wingspan. It can fly at higher altitudes than the Predator B. The Altair also has systems that allow it to safely share airspace with piloted aircraft.

The Altair made its first flight in June 2003. In the future, scientists may use the Altair to help them view forest fires, volcanoes, or dangerous weather conditions.

The MQ-1 Predator

Function:	Target Acquisition
Manufacturer:	General Atomics Aeronautical Systems Inc.
Date First Deployed:	2001
Length:	27 feet (8.2 meters)
Wingspan:	48.7 feet (14.8 meters)
Maximum Weight:	2,250 pounds (1,020 kilograms)
Engine:	Rotax 914 gasoline engine
Top Speed:	170 miles (274 kilometers) per hour
Maximum Altitude:	25,000 feet (7,620 meters)
Maximum Flying Endurance:	40 hours

1 Nose

2 Camera system

3 Wing

4 Stabilizer

5 Inverted V-tail

6 Line-of-sight data link

7 Hellfire II missile

8 Propeller

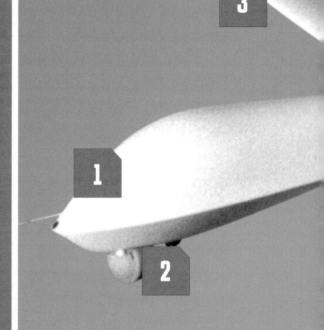

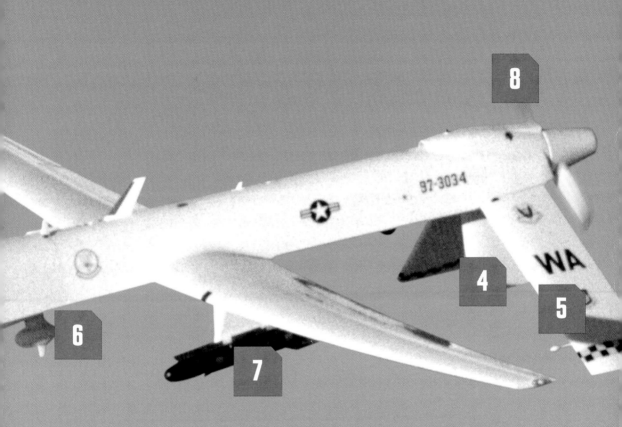

97-3034

WA

8

4

5

6

7

CHAPTER 3

Weapons and Tactics

Shortly after the Predator entered service, Air Force officials decided a weapon would make the Predator even more useful. The Air Force equipped the Predator with the Hellfire missile. This missile was first designed for U.S. Army vehicles. Today, the military uses many Hellfire models. The MQ-1 Predator carries the AGM-114K Hellfire II. The aircraft can carry one missile under each wing.

The AGM-114K Hellfire II

Features of the AGM-114K help the Predator on attack missions. The AGM-114K weighs about 100 pounds (45 kilograms). It is about 5 feet (1.5 meters) long. The top range of the AGM-114K is about 5 miles (8 kilometers).

Predator MQ-1s can carry one missile under each wing.

97-3034

W.

LEARN ABOUT:

Hellfire II missile parts

HEAT warheads

MQ-1 laser seeker

Several sections make up the AGM-114K. They include the motor, control, and warhead sections. The motor section is located at the missile's rear. It allows the missile to reach speeds of up to 950 miles (1,529 kilometers) an hour.

The control section moves four fins at the back of the missile. The fins keep the missile on course.

The warhead is behind the missile's nose. It contains two high-explosive antitank (HEAT) warheads. These explosives are powerful enough to go through vehicles with strong metal armor.

The laser seeker in the AGM-114K's nose finds laser light on a target. It allows the missile to follow the beam of light.

The features of the AGM-114K make it a useful weapon for the Predator and other military aircraft.

Hellfire Autopilot System

The AGM-114K Hellfire II has a built-in autopilot system. If the laser light on the target moves, the system keeps the laser seeker aimed in the direction of the target. It can help the laser seeker find the target again.

New Predator models, such as the MQ-9, also will carry Hellfire II missiles.

The autopilot system also keeps the missile flying at a low altitude. Cloudy and foggy conditions can cause the laser seeker to lose track of its target. These weather conditions are less common at low altitudes than they are at high altitudes.

CHAPTER 4

The Future

Air Force officials are happy with the Predator's performance in recent wars and conflicts. They have decided to buy more advanced Predators. The Air Force also wants other remotely piloted aircraft in the future.

MQ-9

GA-ASI developed a new Predator for the Air Force in 1999. It is called the Predator B, or the MQ-9. The Air Force began testing the MQ-9 in 2001. The Air Force currently has three MQ-9s. Air Force officials plan to have more MQ-9s in the future.

The Air Force plans to fly MQ-9s on future missions.

LEARN ABOUT:

Future Predator plans

MQ-9 features

New remotely piloted aircraft

The MQ-9 has many improvements over the MQ-1. A larger, more powerful engine helps it fly faster and higher than the MQ-1. The MQ-9 can reach speeds of at least 230 miles (370 kilometers) per hour. It can reach an altitude of more than 45,000 feet (13,716 meters). The MQ-9's larger size allows it to carry more equipment.

The Global Hawk is the largest remotely piloted aircraft ever built.

Global Hawk

The Air Force plans to use other remotely piloted aircraft in the future. Northrop Grumman produces the Global Hawk for the Air Force. The Global Hawk is the largest remotely piloted aircraft ever built. The aircraft is 44 feet (13 meters) long and has a wingspan of 116 feet (35 meters). It can carry 2,000 pounds (907 kilograms) of reconnaissance equipment. The Global Hawk can take pictures of land areas as large as 50,000 square miles (129,500 square kilometers).

The Air Force first flew the Global Hawk in 1998. Pilots flew several Global Hawk missions during Operation Enduring Freedom (2001). Northrop Grumman plans to produce Global Hawks until about 2013.

X-45 UCAV

Boeing is building a remotely piloted aircraft called the X-45 Unmanned Combat Aerial Vehicle (UCAV). The Air Force began testing the X-45 in 2002. The X-45's main role will be to destroy enemy antiaircraft guns on the ground.

The X-45 will be able to find enemy targets on its own. Sensor operators will only need to make sure the target is correct before firing a missile.

In recent years, the Air Force has spent millions of dollars on remotely piloted aircraft. The military respects the role the Predator and other aircraft of its kind play in keeping flight crews safe.

The Air Force began testing the X-45 in 2002.

Glossary

altitude (AL-ti-tude)—height above the ground

armor (AR-mur)—a protective metal covering

autopilot system (AW-toh-pye-luht SISS-tuhm)—a device that automatically controls an aircraft or weapon

laser beam (LAY-zur BEEM)—a narrow, intense beam of light

mission (MISH-uhn)—a military task

radar (RAY-dar)—equipment that uses radio waves to locate objects

reconnaissance mission (re-KAH-nuh-suhnss MISH-uhn)—a military mission to gain information about an enemy

satellite dish (SAT-uh-lite DISH)—a round device that receives electronic signals

throttle (THROT-uhl)—a control that allows pilots to increase or decrease the plane's speed

warhead (WOR-hed)—the explosive part of a missile or rocket

Read More

Holden, Henry M. *Air Force Aircraft.* Aircraft. Berkeley Heights, N.J.: Enslow, 2001.

Loves, June. *Military Aircraft.* Flight. Philadelphia: Chelsea House, 2001.

Pace, Steve. *X-Planes: America's Research Aircraft.* St. Paul, Minn.: MBI Publishing, 2003.

Sievert, Terri. *The U.S. Air Force at War.* On the Front Lines. Mankato, Minn.: Capstone Press, 2002.

Useful Addresses

Air Combat Command
Office of Public Affairs
115 Thompson Street, Suite 211
Langley AFB, VA 23665

United States Air Force Museum
1100 Spaatz Street
Wright-Patterson AFB, OH 45433

Internet Sites

FactHound offers a safe, fun way to find Internet sites related to this book. All of the sites on FactHound have been researched by our staff.

Here's how:

1. Visit *www.facthound.com*
2. Type in this special code **0736824170** for age-appropriate sites. Or enter a search word related to this book for a more general search.
3. Click on the **Fetch It** button.

FactHound will fetch the best sites for you!

Index